MW01622805

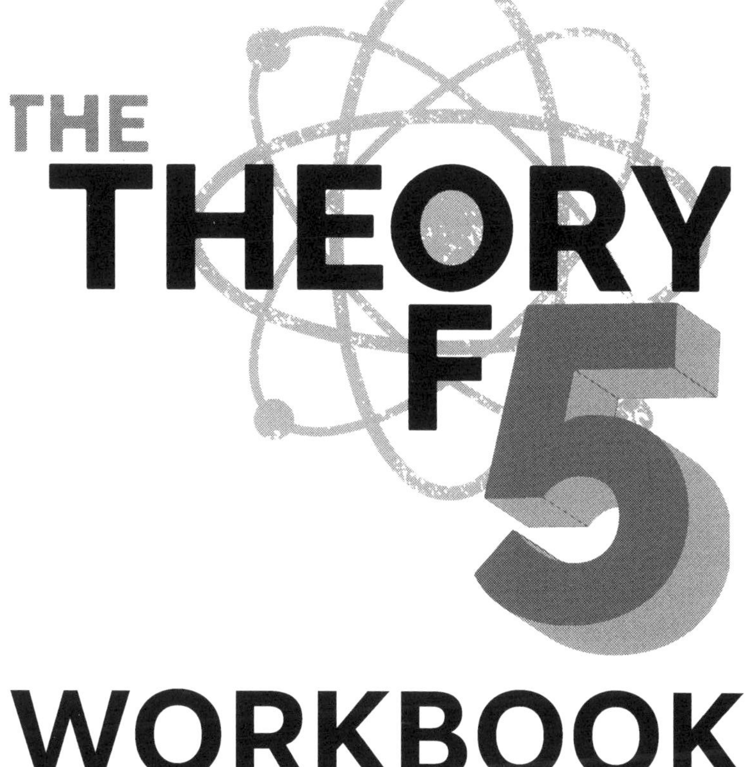
THE
THEORY
F
5
WORKBOOK

Share Your Thoughts and Experiences!

What ideas or concepts from *The Theory of 5* speak to you most strongly? What are you going to take away from this book that you can put into action *today*? Share what excites you with other readers of *The Theory of 5* — or those you know could benefit! Use the **#TheoryOf5** tag for photos or quotes on Twitter, Instagram, Facebook and others and let us know what speaks to you!

Also, connect with us on social media and share your experiences with the author and your Theory of 5 peers:

- Facebook - https://www.facebook.com/CBSaraceno/
- Instagram - @TheoryOf5
- YouTube - https://www.youtube.com/c/theoryof5
- Web - https://www.theoryof5.com

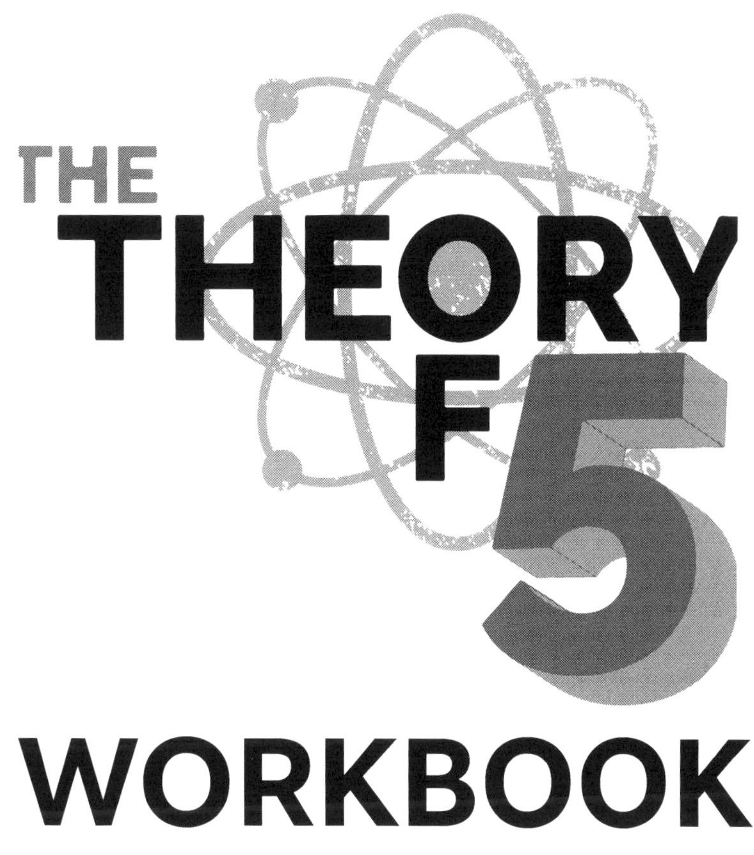

WORKBOOK

Chris Saraceno
with David Falkirk Davis

The Theory of 5 Workbook by Chris Saraceno
with David Falkirk Davis

First Printing, 2018
ISBN 978-1-7323012-3-8

SEL027000 SELF-HELP / Personal Growth / Success
SEL021000 SELF-HELP / Motivational & Inspirational

TABLE OF CONTENTS

This Workbook and How to Use It

The Theory of 5 isn't a passive philosophical discussion. It's not something intended to be read, turned over in your mind a few times as an intellectual exercise and then set aside. The ideas by themselves won't get you the results you desire. They're simply words on a page.

The Theory of 5 is an *active* pursuit — one that will change your life.

In my book *The Theory of 5*, I share with you how this pursuit has changed my life and the lives of those around me who have put this philosophy into action. The cornerstone of the Theory is to find mentors and co-mentors to assist you in the five fundamental areas of your life:

- Religion/spirituality
- Marriage/relationships
- Parenting
- Business and Finance
- Health and Fitness

Because of the guidance, coaching and challenges these mentors will provide, you'll see results that are almost impossible to achieve otherwise. This only works, however, if you put the ideas of The Theory of 5 into *action*.

This workbook is a tool to get you started on your journey. It's designed to take what could be a passive reading experience and actively engage your mind and your heart to generate the results you desire.

How to Use This Book

This workbook is meant to be a companion piece to *The Theory of 5*, not a substitute or a stand-alone book. While some of the questions here could be answered without reading the book, the experience absolutely becomes richer with the context *The Theory of 5* provides. The most effective way to use this workbook, I believe, is to read a chapter of the book, and then answer the questions in the corresponding chapter of this workbook while the reading is still fresh in your mind.

The ideas contained within *The Theory of 5* are examined here, with questions intended to make you think about your personal needs and desires. While I firmly believe that The Theory of 5 will support everyone with achieving their life goals, we all have our unique situations and experiences. By answering the questions in this book, you'll have a better understanding of *your* journey to this point, and the actions, behaviors and attitudes needed in order for you to live your best life.

You will notice that a few of the questions from section to section might seem similar. There are two reasons for this:

- Life isn't easily segmented. Your feelings toward money or the lessons you've taken from your parents, for instance, bleed over into other elements of your life.

- Each section deals with a specific area of life. Look at the questions through that prism; the same question might have different answers depending on this context.

Take an Active Role

Many of our parents told us as children not to write in our books. This is not the case here. With *The Theory of 5 Workbook*, it's *essential* that you write in it. Don't simply answer in your mind and move on; take a pen or pencil and actually write your answers down. The physical act of writing unlocks new ways of thinking.

If you find yourself needing more room for your answers, if you're using the eBook version of this workbook or if you just can't break the deep-set aversion to writing in a book, feel free to use a notebook. The important thing is to commit to writing down every answer.

There might be a temptation to answer with a keyboard, as well, especially if you're a good typist. Avoid this. If you use a keyboard regularly, you can probably type about as fast as you can think. Writing out your answer by hand will be slower, so you'll be forced to slow down your thinking. This is a *good* thing; it will allow you to get to the deeper truths.

Dig Deep

I'll tell you a truth up front: This will not be easy. I promise you it will be *absolutely* worth it, but there will be places you'll visit in your mind along the way that will be uncomfortable. Be prepared for this — and do it anyway.

Your willingness to begin living a Theory of 5 life tells me one thing immediately about you: You're not afraid of a challenge. It's through life's challenges that we grow and learn, and that's what this workbook — and *The Theory of 5* itself — is based upon.

I'm not going to set "rules," but I believe there are three things necessary for you to gain the best results from this workbook and from *The Theory of 5*:

- Answer all the questions in each section without cherry picking the "easy" answers.
- Think deeply about each question; go past the superficial surface and dig into your truth.
- Be honest with yourself.

No one else has to see your answers. You're not writing for an audience or to be graded as if this was a test. You're writing for yourself, and you'll receive the best results if you make the commitment to give all the questions here your full attention and your utmost honesty.

This is It

Your time in this life is finite, and it's up to you to make the most of it. With *The Theory of 5*, you'll build a team around you that will challenge you, guide you and support you in living a life that others only dream of. In this way, you'll provide for yourself and your family and be able to leave a legacy.

That journey starts here, and I can't express enough how excited I am for you and what's to come in your life. Let's get started on your journey!

— Chris Saraceno

Introduction

The Theory of 5: What It Is and How to Use It

When you open your mind to the ideas contained within the pages that follow, you'll find ways to ignite your passions.

You will discover the means and behaviors needed to change your life for the better.

When you adopt The Theory of 5 philosophy, it will become the ultimate playbook for positive transformation and growth within your life.

It All Starts with You

p. 4-5

One of the few absolute truths in this life is that none of us know how long we will live. Do we have decades? Years? Months? Minutes? Another truth is that time can never be replaced or reused. Once it's gone, it's gone. Time is our most precious commodity.

Let's begin our journey to a Theory of 5 life with the end in mind:

For what three things would you like to be most remembered?

1. ______________________________

2. ______________________________

3. ______________________________

To be the best version of you, what are the *skill, habit and attitude* changes you believe you need right now? Why?

____

____

____

____

____

The "Self-Made" Man

p. 6

No matter where we start out in life, we require others to shape us, sharpen us and guide us. While we may find some level of success on our own, we'll never achieve our true potential and discover our best self without assistance and support from other exceptional, motivated people.

Which area of The Theory of 5 needs the most attention in your life right now? Why?

____

____

What other areas of your life would you like to work on?

____

____

How has that changed in the past few years? Do you feel it has improved? How?

____

____

How do you see your life changing in the next few years?

____

____

Seeking, Finding and Asking

p. 7-8

Those who have achieved success and have years of experience and wisdom are often more than happy to guide and teach someone who comes to them with an open attitude *and a* willing heart, *ready to put in the effort. Many times, all we have to do is ask.*

What are some of your go-to, "favorite" excuses?

____

____

____

Who are some people you admire?

____

____

____

What about them *specifically* do you admire?

____

____

____

My Own Path

p. 9-11

The Theory of 5 won't keep us from making mistakes in our lives. It's not a magic spell or a miracle cure for life's setbacks. My mentors have all expressed to me that there have been times when they've felt like they've taken two steps forward and three steps back. This is, no doubt, a familiar feeling to everyone, no matter how successful he or she is. What the Theory does *provide, however, is a framework and a foundation that allows us to thrive in good times and survive the bad.*

What are, or should have been, some of the "wake up" calls in your own life?

What in your life are you most proud of? Why?

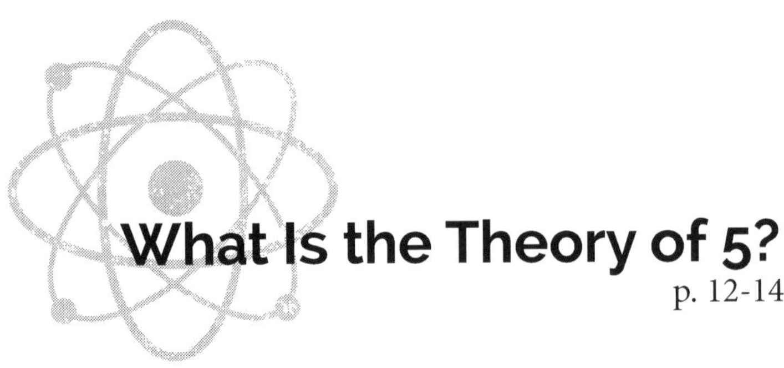

What Is the Theory of 5?

p. 12-14

The Theory, which can be used by anyone at any stage of life, is based on selecting mentors in the five most significant areas of a person's life — spirituality, marriage, parenting, business and finance, and health. *These men and women will guide and support us towards fulfilling our ultimate potential in each area.*

In one sentence for each, describe how you would like to grow in these areas:

Spirituality/Religion ______________________________

____

Marriage/Relationship ______________________________

____

Parenting ______________________________

____

Business/Finance ______________________________

____

Health/Fitness ______________________________

____

Which area of the Theory of 5 is most important to you right now? Why?

____

Who are your five closest personal connections (Circle I) at this moment?

1. ____

2. ____

3. ____

4. ____

5. ____

On a scale of 1 to 10 (1 = extremely negative, 10 = exceptional) rate the positive influence of the members of your Five Personal Connections.

1. ______ 2.. ______ 3.. ______ 4. ______ 5. ______

Who are five people who could be your inspirational connections (Circle II)? What positive inspiration could each give you? (Note: Some of these connections could already be in your personal connection list.)

1. ____

2. ____

3. ____

4. ____

5. ____

In each of the five areas, what two or three qualities are most important for your ideal inspirational connection to have?

Spirituality/Religion ______________________________

____

Marriage/Relationship ______________________________

____

Parenting ______________________________

____

Business/Finance ______________________________

____

Health/Fitness______________________________

____

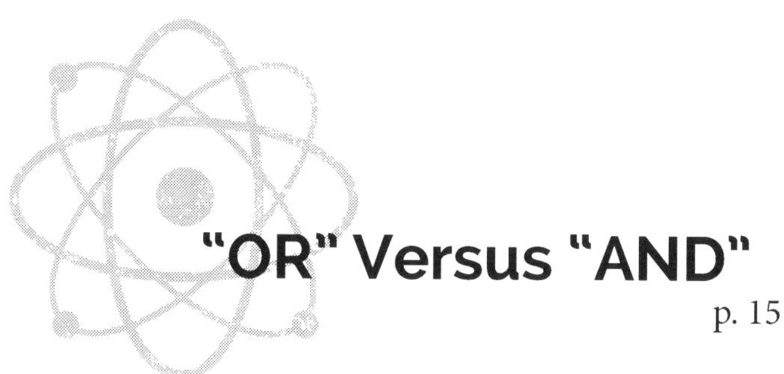

"OR" Versus "AND"

p. 15

Limiting ourselves to certain options before even considering that we could have it all ensures limited results.

What are some contradictory paths in your life that are not actually contradictory when examined using "The Genius of the AND" mindset?

____

____

____

____

____

How has "The Tyranny of the OR" held you back or been the reason behind passed-up opportunities?

____

____

____

____

____

The Time Is NOW

p. 16

People are finding success today like never before — studies show that there are currently 1,700 new millionaires every day, and more than 11 million millionaires in the United States. And prosperity isn't just about money; there are more opportunities than ever to find ways to improve yourself, be true to your calling, to live life on your terms and find your own rewards.

Other than money, what are some other ways you would like to be "rich"?

____

____

____

What are some self-imposed roadblocks holding you back from taking action?

1. ____

2. ____

3. ____

Describe how you can overcome these self-imposed roadblocks. Be *specific.*

1. ____

2. ____

3. ____

The Mentoring Mindset

Preparation and Expectations

Everyone wants to have a happy and prosperous life — to have an existence that matters.

The philosophy behind The Theory of 5 is one everyone can put into action in order to reap rewards. It's easier to achieve our goals when we have the support of those who have accomplished what we've set out to do. It's also important to find those who are like-minded; this allows us to challenge and encourage each other.

The lessons and the ideas presented here strengthen our commitment to pursue the opportunities in areas that matter most to us.

This Book and Your Needs

p. 18

We all come to the table with different skills, different experiences and different goals. None of the five elements of the Theory are more important than the others — as stated previously, it depends on where we are, what we want and what we need in our lives at any given moment.

Which of the five areas are you strongest in right now? Why?

____

____

____

Which of the five areas do you need the most work? Why?

____

____

____

What are some "goals" you might have for your life that actually come from others' expectations?

____

____

____

A Word Before Beginning (The Author's Mindset)

p. 19-21

In addition to giving me practical lessons on how best to harness my time and energy, they also opened my mind to the idea that I didn't have to do it alone.

What is your "Why" in life? Be specific.

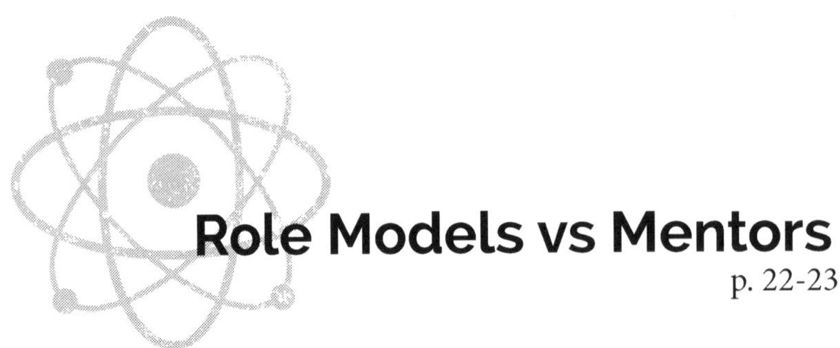

Role Models vs Mentors

p. 22-23

We may receive guidance in one area from someone while providing them guidance in an area in which we're stronger. These are the relationships that enrich everyone's lives, and where The Theory of 5 really comes to life

Who are some role models from history you most admire? Why?

____

____

Name three co-mentors you either have or could have in your life right now.

1. ______________________________________

2. ______________________________________

3. ______________________________________

Look at the list of the areas you found you need to work on in the "Self-Made Man" section of this workbook (p. 5) — what do you believe you need that would support your growth in these areas?

____

____

____

Leave Your Ego at the Door

p. 24-25

Most of us are familiar with the statement, "Pride cometh before the fall" — and no truer words have ever been written. We're all ignorant about something. There's no shame in accepting that. What is *a shame is when someone is too proud to admit it — when they're too proud to ask for training, advice or education.*

What thinking or behaviors are holding you back? How will you improve this?

____

____

____

What strength or talent do you hide or run away from? Why?

____

____

____

What new technology or other lesson would you like to learn? Who could teach you?

____

____

____

The Anti-Mentor

p. 26-29

While mentors can provide us with the blueprints of how to succeed in any facet of life, there's another valuable resource that we shouldn't ignore. We can also learn from the bad examples of others. Many times, learning what not *to do is as important as learning what we should do.*

What bad behaviors did/do the anti-mentors in your own life model that you want to commit to not duplicating?

____

____

What are you most afraid of? How can you use this fear as motivation?

Fear: ____

Motivation: ____

For each of your anti-mentors, find at least one thing positive about them.

____

____

What can you forgive them for? How could forgiving them support your growth?

____

____

Programming Our Onboard Computer

p. 30-32

The most successful people I've met have learned to program their onboard computers with positive questions. Because of this, the answers they receive move them forward because positive questions produce positive answers.

Pay attention to your "inner monologue" today. Are there questions you regularly ask yourself framed in a positive or negative way? Are the comments you make to yourself helpful or hurtful? List some of your regular monologue questions here.

____

____

____

____

Practice FIVE positive questions to yourself for one week. Write them here.

1. ____
2. ____
3. ____
4. ____
5. ____

Removing Self-Limitations

p. 33-36

These are the people who avoid "mistakes" at all costs. Mistakes can poke holes in the "all-knowing" image they hold of themselves, so they never risk trying anything new. They fear looking "foolish" or anything other than perfect. The truth is that it's okay to make mistakes. Mistakes show that we're trying to master something new to us. They are a sign of growth and striving to become more tomorrow than we are today.

Name a situation when you could have learned something but didn't because you didn't want to be seen as "uncertain" or "uneducated."

____

____

____

____

____

Think about a time when you learned from a failure.
Compare the fear you felt to the reality of the situation.

____

____

____

____

Think of a time when you believe you "should have" done more but didn't. What was the result? What do you think the result would have been with a little more effort?

Be anything but average: What are some areas of your life that would benefit from just a little extra action, attention and focus?

Give Back and Pay It Forward

p. 37-38

We all need to look out for ourselves in this world; that's a given. After all, with the possible exception of our parents or other loved ones, no one will care as much about our success as we do. When self-interest is all we care about, though, that's a sad, short-sighted, debilitating attitude to hold. Compassion is a strong trait of The Theory of 5.

In what areas could you be a mentor for someone else?
Where can you make a difference in someone's life?

What steps can you take today to enable you to be the best mentor you can be?

Who in your life have you shown love to today? How have you shown it?

Taking the First Step

p. 39

By living a Theory of 5 lifestyle — and that's what it is, a lifestyle, not a bandage or a shortcut — you are about to separate yourself from the pack. You will stay ahead by consistently taking action. Where others give up, you will get *up and keep going.*

Dream BIG! What are three long-term goals you'd like to achieve that might seem impossible for you today?

1. ______________________________

____

____

____

2. ______________________________

____

____

____

3. ______________________________

____

____

____

Finding Spirituality That Works for Us

Defining our spirituality is a lifelong process. It's not something we can "accomplish"; there is no finish line.

We don't have to walk this path alone, though. People are willing to share and assist us on our spiritual journeys. Some even feel called to do so. It's a matter of finding the right people to support and guide us — and to challenge us when necessary.

These are the individuals who will be there to consistently raise our standards and remind us of our purpose: to grow and become the best version of ourselves.

Finding Our Place In a Larger World

p. 42

With a spiritual and moral framework in place, our decisions become easier to make. Those decisions might not be easy to live out — doing the right thing can often be more difficult than what might feel good in the moment — but they provide peace of mind that would otherwise be difficult to achieve.

What are some areas in your life where you feel responsible for, even though you have no real control over them? Why?

The Author's Journey

p. 43-45

My mentors and I believe it's critical for us to ask the important questions and see ourselves as a part of a larger world. That need is universal, and that's the main thrust of what we'll be discussing here.

What religious and/or spiritual teachings were you raised with, if any?

How close do you feel to those teachings today? How do you differ?

What role does spirituality play in your everyday life? During times of stress?

Our Focus in Life

p. 46

When hit with life's setbacks or heartbreak — as we all will experience in our lives — people without the larger worldview that spirituality provides often have nothing to fall back upon.

What are some everyday benefits you believe spirituality can bring — or does bring —to your life?

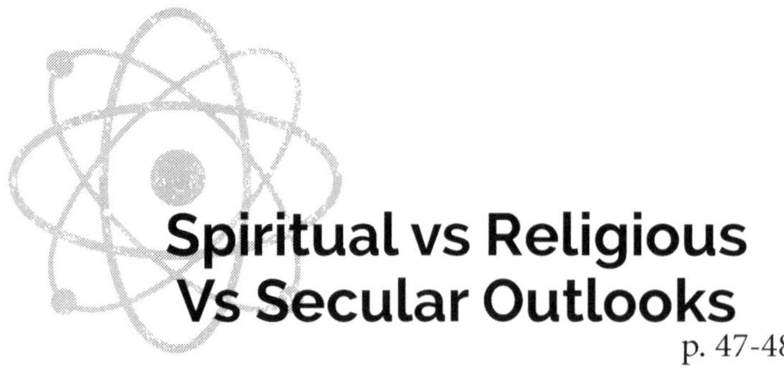

Spiritual vs Religious Vs Secular Outlooks

p. 47-48

Cold logic does not and cannot *give most people comfort; from the spiritual perspective, there's more to life than just the things we look at every day.*

In what specific instances of your life has (or would have) a spiritual outlook been better/more productive/more comforting than a strictly secular outlook?

When has the idea of total control been an illusion for you?
How did you feel when the illusion fell away?

How do you deal with "unfair" moments in life?

When Tragedy Strikes

p. 49

Even when the pain digs deeper than we believed possible, even when heartache alters the tapestry of our family, spirituality can give us the lifeline we can use to pull through these times. Many of us rely on spiritual messages and ideas to lead us to calmer waters and greener pastures of hope

When have you been given comfort during a stressful/heartbreaking time?

____

____

____

____

What kind of support did you want/need the most? Why did you need this?

____

____

____

When have you given support to another? Be specific.

____

____

____

Finding Our Flock

p. 50-51

No one goes to church — or any presentation for that matter — to be bored. Some may show up out of duty or habit, but people want to be excited.

If you attend a church, what do you find most valuable?

____

____

____

If you do not attend a church, what kind of spiritual experience do you enjoy or would you most like? Why is this important to you?

____

____

____

What moves you the most in a religious and/or spiritual setting?

____

____

____

Iron Sharpens Iron

p. 52-54

If a mentor actually cares about our well being and spiritual progress, they will tell us when we're falling short. While it might be difficult to hear — our first impulse might be to become defensive — good mentors will ask the tough questions.

What information would you find most valuable to receive from an accountability mentor?

What are some of your activities that could be seen as inspiring to others? What *will* you do to share your inspiring activities or message?

Name an experience when you would have been better served to admit a mistake, learn from it and find a way not to repeat it. Be specific.

Name two people who you know would be valuable face-to-face mentors. Why would they be good people to fill this vital role in your life?

1. ______________________________

Why? ______________________________

2. ______________________________

Why? ______________________________

Who are two virtual mentors who would be valuable to you? Why?

1. ______________________________

Why? ______________________________

2. ______________________________

Why? ______________________________

Being completely honest with yourself, are you ready to be as accountable to others as you are to have others be accountable to you?
If not, what steps can you take to get yourself to that point?

____

____

____

____

Do you have a favorite spiritual quote? Do you live by that quote? If so, how?

____

____

____

Our Monday-Through-Saturday Path

p. 55

...it's easier on a Sunday to think about and preach about The 10 Commandments than it is to live them during the week. This is why it's so important to surround ourselves with good people in all aspects of our life.

What are some areas in your life where you live up to your beliefs, no matter what?

What are some areas where you know you could improve?

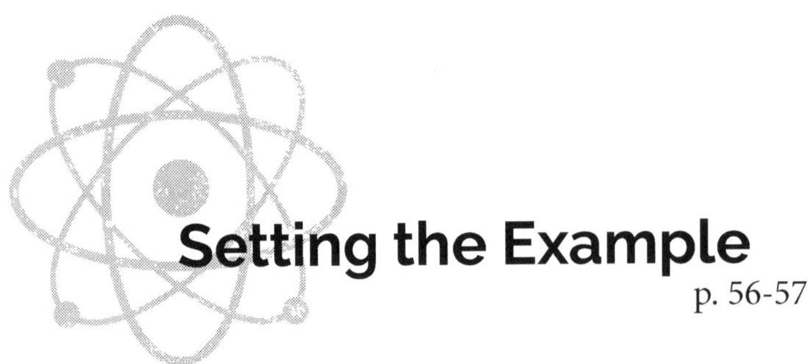

Setting the Example

p. 56-57

Parents must encourage their children to see challenges as opportunities for growth, and not obstacles standing in the way of what they want.

How were you introduced to religion and/or spirituality as a child (if you were)? Was it effective? Was it fun? Was it punishing? What experience did you take from it?

What impact are you having on the children in your life in this area?

What are the spiritual tools you want the children in your life to have as they mature?

What tools do you wish you would have had growing up? Do you have them now?

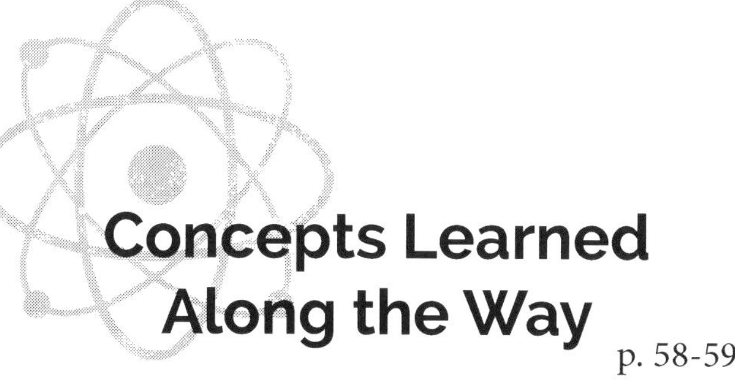

Concepts Learned Along the Way

p. 58-59

Pride keeps us from learning the lessons we need to learn and asking for guidance when we need it the most.

How do you serve others? Do you do it comfortably? Why or why not?

What are some incidents of your own pride getting in the way of your own best interests? What is your reasoning for this attitude?

Putting the Lessons Into Practice in Business

p. 60

By truly being concerned for their team — not faking it with hollow platitudes — true leaders can create a sense of unity and family within their team.

Do you have *true* leadership at your business/work? Explain your answer.

____

____

____

____

If you are a leader, what are some areas in which you excel and areas where you fall short? How can you improve?

____

____

____

____

____

Taking Stock

p. 61

We have to keep an open dialogue with ourselves, checking in and digging deep to see if we're meeting the goals we know *we're capable of attaining.*

What are some of your long-term spiritual goals?

Why are they important to you?

What are some short-, mid- and long-term steps can you take to reach these goals?

A Marriage of Equals

A truly happy and prosperous relationship provides us with a pool of strength we can use to deal with whatever life throws at us.

Knowing we have the support of a life partner will allow us to overcome whatever obstacle we might encounter or give us the stamina to endure the unavoidable.

Also, life is just more fun *when we can share our dreams, hopes and worldly possessions with someone we love and appreciate — and who feels the same about us.*

"What's Left" Vs "What's Deserved"

p. 64-65

The happiest people I know have mastered the skill of building relationships with their spouse or partner. More than simply being a partner or lover, they are each other's friend.

What are some areas where you feel particularly in sync with your partner?

____

____

____

What are some areas where you believe you take your partner for granted?

____

____

____

What are some areas where you communicate particularly well with your partner?

____

____

____

What are some topics you avoid with your partner at all costs?

What actions have you taken that you felt were mis-judged by your partner? What actions by them have you mis-judged? Compare.

Name a time you've thought about doing something for your partner and then, for whatever reason, didn't. Does this happen often? Why?

The 10 Elements of a Successful Relationship

p. 66-70

For many of us, it's not easy to live up to each of these expectations daily — but it's important to keep them in mind. That's why mentors/co-mentors are so important for maintaining our focus and challenging us to constantly strive to be better. Iron sharpens iron.

1. Love — Do you believe you and your partner demonstrate your love well enough for you? Ask your partner and take note of their answer — truly listen.

____

____

____

____

2. Commitment — How has your relationship evolved over the time you've known each other?

____

____

____

____

3. **Respect** — Describe the division of labor in your relationship. What does your partner "wow" you with, and what do you "wow" them with?

4. **Support** — What have been some of the highs and lows in your life since you've been with your partner? Have they been there for you to celebrate/support? Have you been there for them?

5. **Humor** —How does your partner make you laugh? Words? Actions? How do you make them laugh?

6. **Communication** — When was the last "check in" discussion you've had with your partner? Are you each comfortable telling each other the truth about your feelings?

7. Patience — What specifically would you miss the most about your partner if he/ she were no longer with you?

___

___

___

8. Common Core Values — What is the biggest point of disagreement you have with your partner? How does that affect you? How does it affect your relationship?

___

___

___

9. Forgiveness — Are there any grudges you or your partner hold onto? What would it take to let it go?

___

___

___

___

10. Gratitude — Describe ways you show your appreciation and gratitude to your partner for things they do, both large and small.

___

___

___

___

Mistakes Made and Lessons Learned

p. 71-74

It's ironic that something as important as our relationship with our spouse or partner can be taken for granted. This doesn't have *to be the case for us though. Even if it doesn't come easy for us, there are people who can guide us in building a healthy, kind, loving, exceptional relationship.*

Think back to prior relationships in your life and honestly judge what negative things happened. How much was your doing? Do you see any patterns? If so, be specific.

____

____

____

____

____

____

Are there areas of your life that you focus on so much that you damage or neglect your relationship with your spouse/significant other?

____

____

____

How has what you find attractive in a partner changed over the years? What has remained the same?

What are some areas in your relationship that might appear to work against you "on paper"? How do you make sure you stay strong? What else could you be doing?

What are some of your personal blind spots — areas you neglect if you don't focus?

When was the last time you forgave your partner?

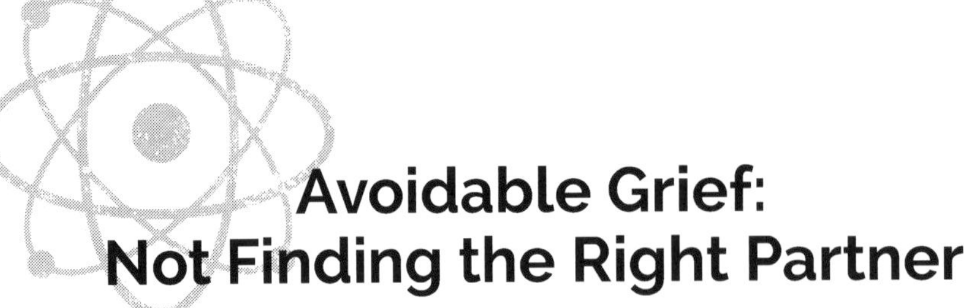

Avoidable Grief: Not Finding the Right Partner

p. 75

The idea that "love conquers all" is certainly a strong notion. There are discussions that need to take place, however, before reception halls are booked and rings are exchanged.

What were some "red flags" in past relationships that you ignored that later became big deals?

____

____

____

____

____

What are some warning signs you now know to avoid in order to make better choices?

____

____

____

____

Life's Big Questions

p. 76-88

Some of these discussions might not take a lot of thought, while others may make a couple reconsider their entire relationship. It's critical to have them, though.

Money

What is each of your financial "styles" (spender, saver, etc)? How does this work in your relationship? Where can it cause friction and what are some ways you can minimize that friction?

Where can you loosen/tighten up? Where can your partner?

Do you share similar financial goals? Describe them.

Values

What values are most important to you in your life? What are your partner's core values? Are they in alignment?

Have your and/or your partner's values evolved over the years? How so?

Religion/Spirituality

Describe the role that religion/spirituality plays in your life. Does it mesh with your partner's? How integral is it to your self-identity? To theirs?

Do you make compromises about religion/spirituality with your partner? How does it work for you?

Living Arrangements

Sit down with your partner and ask them about specifics on your living arrangements (location, career path, housing, education, family, pets and other specifics). Are you in harmony? Have your opinions/desires changed since you first got together?

Are there ongoing stresses that could be solved/eased with better planning?

Division of Labor

Describe the actual or planned division of labor in your household. Is there anything important going undone? Are there areas that need to be re-negotiated and/or discussed?

How have you updated your internal programming when it comes to gender roles?

Intimacy

Are there areas you'd like to discuss regarding intimacy with your partner but are afraid/uncomfortable to bring up? Why?

What are your and your partner's intimacy styles? How can you both satisfy these styles while remaining true to your own?

How has the intimate element of your relationship evolved over the years? Are your and your partner's needs being met?

Children

Have you had the discussion about children with your partner? Any surprises? Are your goals compatible?

Extended Family

What is your extended family situation? Do you wish you lived closer or father apart? What steps can you take to improve this situation?

Do you or your partner have issues with setting boundaries when it comes to family?

Are there family members with issues (moral/financial/health/addiction, etc.) who can or do cause conflict with your partner? How can you best fulfill your responsibilities and still support your partner?

Fighting Fairly and Disagreeing Well

p. 89-93

No matter how compatible they are, two people living together are going to butt heads every now and again, so let's decide on our "rules of engagement" early on. . . . It's tremendously helpful if both parties go into disagreements with the proper mindset.

What are your specific styles when it comes to conflict and what are your partner's? How are these alike? How are they different? How have they evolved over the years?

Recall an argument that didn't go well. What strategies did you use that didn't serve either of you? What strategies did your partner use? What would you improve?

What are some common disagreements where the outcome is important? Which disagreements can you let go of and defer to your partner?

The End (?)

p. 94-95

If reconciliation isn't possible, it's time to settle and move quickly. Once the final decision is made, the longer it takes, the more complicated things will get.

If you've been divorced or had a long-term relationship end, where did things go wrong? Could they have been changed or gone differently, or were there deeper issues that were ultimately insurmountable?

If there were children involved, how were they affected?
What steps could have been taken at the time? What steps can be taken *today*?

Do you carry scars or resentments? If so, how can you get past them? Be specific.

Getting Guidance and Learning from Others

p. 96

Find older couples who have been through life's highs and lows and are still each other's best friends. We can often tell these couples by the little things: their body language, their communication styles and the little gestures that show they still love and care for each other.

What was your parent's relationship like? What can you take from that? What should you leave behind?

____

____

____

____

____

What challenges did they face? How are they alike and different from your own?

____

____

____

____

____

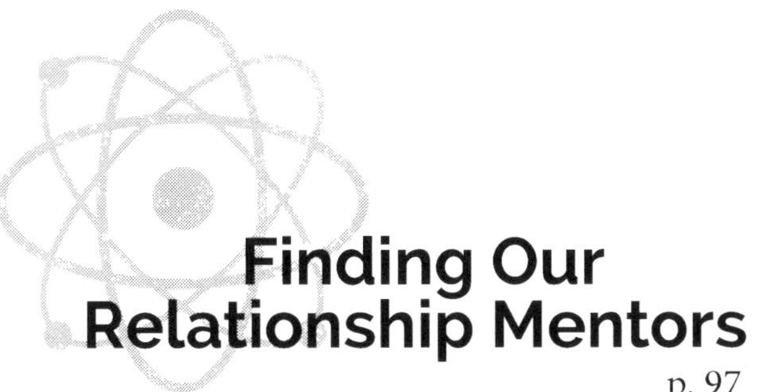

Finding Our Relationship Mentors

p. 97

There are married couples all around us, but from which ones should we seek advice?

Which couple has the relationship you admire the most? Why do you admire them?

___

___

___

What are some of the *little* things you admire and would like to duplicate?

___

___

___

What questions can you ask that would provide answers for your own relationship?

___

___

___

___

Becoming a Mentor

p. 98

Part of the pleasure of finding a mentor is preparing ourselves for the day when we can become one ourselves, to give back to the world what we've received. It's an important duty and opportunity, one where we must be honest and transparent with ourselves before helping another.

Have you ever helped someone try to stay together in their relationship? How did it turn out? What did you learn?

Why would you be a good mentor to another couple in the future?

What can you work on in your own relationship to be a better mentor to others?

The Power of Parenting

The Theory of 5's point of view is that once we become a parent or involved in raising a child, the main goal is to nurture, guide and influence our child to be a respectful, productive, self-sufficient adult.

In order to do this, we have to ensure they have the knowledge, skills, attitudes and behaviors they will need to thrive on their own.

Preparing children to be adults who make a positive difference in the world is a job — and a privilege — where many people may lend a hand.

Our Gift to Society

p. 100

Raising a well-adjusted, highly contributing person is the ultimate gift to a society. While we can't control how other children are raised, however, we are utterly and ultimately responsible for how we raise our own.

Besides your own children (if you have them), name other children who you are involved with in your life.

____

____

____

____

____

In general, what type of effect do you want to have on the children in your life? What specifically do you want them to take from you and your examples?

____

____

____

____

____

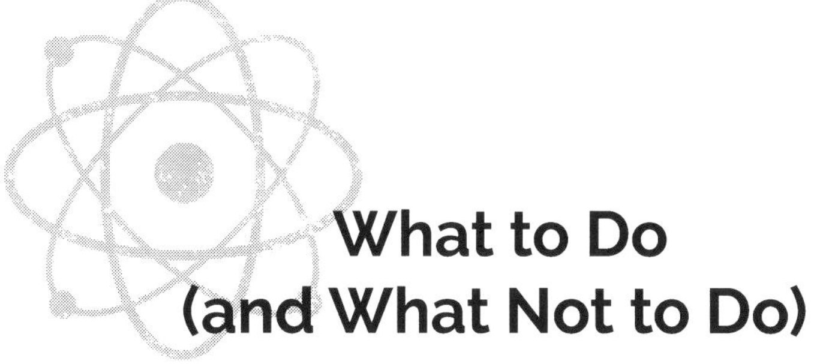

What to Do (and What Not to Do)

p. 101

We want to take advice and be open to the suggestions of parents who have raised healthy, happy, independent children who turn into prosperous adults.

Who are some of your "all-star" parents — past or present — that you'd like to emulate?

Who are some of your "peer" parents? Are they good co-mentors?

What are some "new" challenges that you face today that your own parents did not?

The Guiding Principle

p. 102

The main responsibility of every parent is to successfully set each child up to excel in life with the skills, knowledge, education and life skills necessary to be independent *and* thrive.

What do you think a child should know — both practically and as life skills — by the time they turn 18? What type of lessons would serve them best?

What is your plan for helping them learn these lessons?

Eight Traits to Parenting Success

p. 103-105

Children are learning machines; at some level, nothing *we do goes unnoticed, even in those times when we'd swear no one is listening to us.*

What are some recurring "patience" cases in your relationship with your children? How can you deepen your patience?

___

___

___

What challenges have you faced where the line between "parent" and "friend" blurred? What was the result?

___

___

___

What are some "bedrock" behaviors you'd like to instill in your child, or have instilled in your child?

___

___

___

How do you handle the inevitable "battle of wills" with your child? What have you found effective? What needs work?

What is your philosophy on punishment? Does it work?

Describe your communication style with your children. Is it effective?

Proper Motivation

p. 106

When a child never *moves from extrinsic motivation to intrinsic — whether they are unable or unwilling to do so — they are being set up for failure in life.*

Look back on your answers to "The Guiding Principle" questions (p. 60). How have you moved (or plan to move) your children from extrinsic to intrinsic motivation on important behaviors? Be specific.

Real Love is Tough Love

p. 107

We are holding the child accountable, but we're not doing it out of meanness or indifference. We're doing it because we love them, and we want the best for them.

What are some situations in your own life where tough love has come into play?
Was it effective? Why or why not?

____

____

____

____

____

What "tough love" situations with children have worked for you?
How did the situation resolve? How could the experience have been improved?

____

____

____

____

____

Equal Treatment of Unequals

p. 108-109

Parents who teach their children early on that actions have consequences — *both positive and negative — are training their children to live in the real world. They are giving them the tools they need to succeed.*

Describe a time when you were treated “equally”when the situation really didn't call for it. How did it make you feel?

____

____

____

____

Does your child need extra attention in an area where his or her sibling doesn't? How can you best address the needs of *all* your children?

____

____

____

____

____

____

Parenting is a Joint Venture

p. 110-111

...it's not necessary for each parent to act in lockstep with the other. Different people bring different talents and different temperaments to the table.

How is your parenting style different from your partner's?

When there are times/areas where you don't agree with your partner? How do you deal with it? Is there room for improvement in this discussion?

Adult Children and the Blame Game

p. 112-115

Many children who had difficult childhoods fail to recognize that their parents were mortal. They were flesh-and-blood beings who made mistakes but did the best they could with the tools they had.

What were/are some positive traits of your parents?

____

____

____

What are some old grudges you hold onto from childhood?

____

____

____

How have these grudges affected your life?
List specific reasons why it would benefit you to let go of them.

____

____

____

____

Steps

p. 116-117

They might never say it, but children crave stability, structure and discipline in their lives. Going back and forth between warring households may make the children grow up too fast to protect themselves or might prevent them from ever *maturing to the point of self-sufficiency.*

If you're in a step-parenting situation, describe the atmosphere of both parenting houses. Where are they similar and where do they differ?

____

____

____

____

____

Describe the relationship of the stepparent to the child and the other parent(s) in each house. What could be better? How could this best be achieved?

____

____

____

____

____

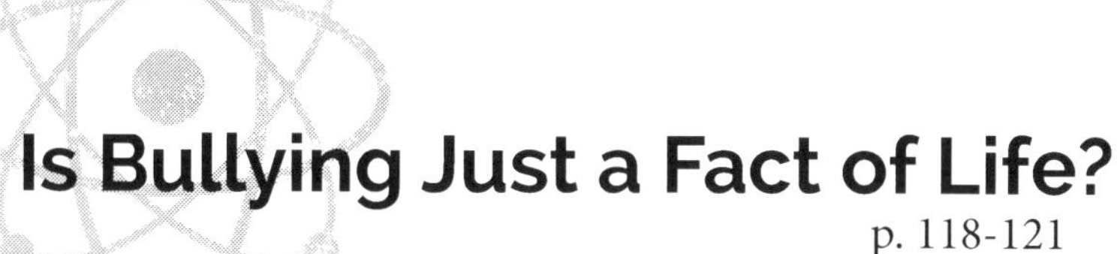

Is Bullying Just a Fact of Life?

p. 118-121

It's crucial to teach our children how to take a joke or handle teasing within reason. We should be prepared to step in, however, when we see our child has become a target of unrelenting bullies.

Think of a situation when you were bullied, or when you, perhaps, were a bully. What advice would you give your younger self now that you have an adult's perspective?

____

____

____

____

What are some skills you'd like to teach your children that would serve them well when it comes to standing up for themselves?

____

____

____

____

____

The Danger of Overprotection

p. 122

College is full of 18-year-old men and women who have no clue *how to balance a checkbook, do their laundry or dishes, or how to cook or clean. They have trouble imagining how their actions will affect them in the future because they don't know how to think beyond their day-to-day life.*

Where are some areas that you might need to step back and let your child learn some lessons on their own?

____

____

____

____

____

Do you feel you are getting your children ready for life? Explain, and be specific.

____

____

____

____

____

The Positive Aspect of Failure

p. 123

As we get older, we acquire profound knowledge — we know what's going to happen if our children don't listen. But there are moments when we have to sit back, give our advice and then just watch.

Name a time in your own life where failure actually set you up for later success.

____

____

____

____

How should you support your child through a failure without robbing them of that failure's lesson?

____

____

____

____

Sharing Our Own Struggles

p. 124

They'll have challenges in life to overcome; it will benefit them to know how their parents overcame their own obstacles.

You are really your children's first mentor, just as your parents were your own.
What struggles of your parents have supported your growth?
What do you wish you would have known about them as a child that you now know?

List some struggles you overcame that will provide your children with valuable lessons

Life's Not Fair

p. 125-126

As children, we have few choices during our first few years. As we become teenagers and adults, however, our choices become almost unlimited.

What are some of the privileges your child has that he or she didn't earn on their own?

____

____

____

What are some of obstacles they face that are no fault of their own?

____

____

____

What are you doing to enhance their passion, future and character without making it too easy for them?

____

____

____

Respecting Our Children's Differences

p. 127

To get the best results, we need to tailor our responses and actions to our child's personality. While we want the same outcome for each — to be productive, happy, capable adults — we might need to take a slightly different approach for each child to ultimately reach that goal.

What are two or three ways your children are different from each other?

____

____

____

What are their individual strengths and opportunities for growth?

____

____

____

How are their communication styles different from each other?

____

____

____

Benevolent Brainwashing

p. 128-129

By letting them know we did these things because we loved them, the lessons had a better chance of taking hold. These are the lessons they'll remember and value as adults, and eventually pass along to their own children.

What statements did you grow up with? How did they impact your mindset as you matured?

___

___

___

What are some of your family's current mottoes or sayings?

___

___

___

___

What values do these mottoes instill?
Do your children know them by heart and the meaning behind them?

___

___

Discipline and Anger

p. 130-131

Children will *make us angry — it's going to happen. How we react, however, will set the tone for what's to come.*

What is your philosophy on discipline? Does this instill in them that their actions have positive/negative consequences? If not, how could you adjust this discipline?

____

____

____

What are some of your "go to" punishments? Are they effective?
Could a different approach be more effective?

____

____

____

Do you ever commit to overly long punishments that actually punish *you?*
If so, what would be more effective long-term punishments to use?

____

____

____

The Trust Tree

p. 132

It takes much more effort to build trust than it does to break it. Once someone's trust in us is lost, it is not easily regained. It takes a lot of work to rebuild it to the point where it was before we let that person down.

Describe a time in your life where you fell short of the trust someone close to you had in you. How did you regain that trust? If you *didn't* regain their trust, what would you do differently knowing what you know today?

____

____

____

____

Do you have a family motto/analogy about truth? If so, what is it?
If you don't, find or design one and write it down now.

____

____

____

____

____

Their Side of Things

p. 133

By allowing the child to feel "heard," even if the decision ultimately goes against what they want, we can build respect. We can strengthen our relationship with them and sometimes short-circuit an issue before it gets blown out of proportion.

Is there a time when you jumped to the wrong conclusion in a discussion with your child? How do you think this made them feel?

What questions will you ask in the future to avoid misunderstandings?

The Good Times

p. 134-135

We're at our best when we take the time to create great memories for life. Never underestimate the importance of fun, humor, laughing and special one-on-one time with our child.

What are some of your favorite memories of your own childhood?

What are some of your favorite places or activities with your children? Plan five special one-on-one memories with your child/niece/nephew or other child in your life.

1.

2.

3.

4.

5.

What is something you haven't done that you think you and your family would enjoy and have fond memories of as they grow older?

Do you have a strong sense of how much praise is appropriate?
Do you ever under- or over-praise them? How do you think this will impact them?

The Time Machine Mentality

p. 136-137

When the decisions get hard and the energy gets low, looking at our present situation by imagining our future can reframe the discussion. It can help us keep our eyes on our ultimate goal of raising self-sufficient adults we can be proud of and who are proud of themselves.

Imagine that your 30-year-old self is standing next to you.
What do you think he/she would say to you?

Imagine your grown child next to you.
What would he/she thank you for? What regrets would you or they have?

Teaching Money Management

p. 138-139

No matter what our net worth, we can leave a financial legacy to our children — a legacy that will have an incredible impact on their financial future.

What do you wish your parents would have taught you about money?

For better or worse, how have your parents lessons/examples impacted your current financial state?

What specific financial lessons do you believe are the most important to teach children?

Little Things That Make a Big Difference

p. 140

Children aren't born knowing these rules and behaviors. They must be modeled by the parent who recognizes the worth of a great first impression.

What elements are most important to you when it comes to first impressions, both what you strive to put forward and what you expect from others? Why?

What are some examples of manners you believe are most important? Why? How are you teaching these vital lessons to your children?

No One Thing

p. 141

Being a parent is an awesome opportunity but also an awesome responsibility. The steps we take now and the effort we put in while they grow up makes the difference between someone who'll take on the world and win and someone who will be victimized by everything that comes their way.

What are two or three small things your parents did for you or around you that shaped you into the person you eventually become?

What are two or three small things you do with your own children today that they will look back at one day and find were important?

Finding Your Circle

p. 142

As much as we'd like to believe that we, as parents, have the ultimate *influence on children, though, we also know other people will play a part in their development. The people our children associate with on a daily basis will directly impact their beliefs, thoughts, opinions and actions in the future.*

Who are your children's best friends? Are they good influences? Why or why not?

____

____

____

Are *your* best friends good influences on you? Why or why not?

____

____

____

Are *you* a good influence on your circle? Why or why not?

____

____

____

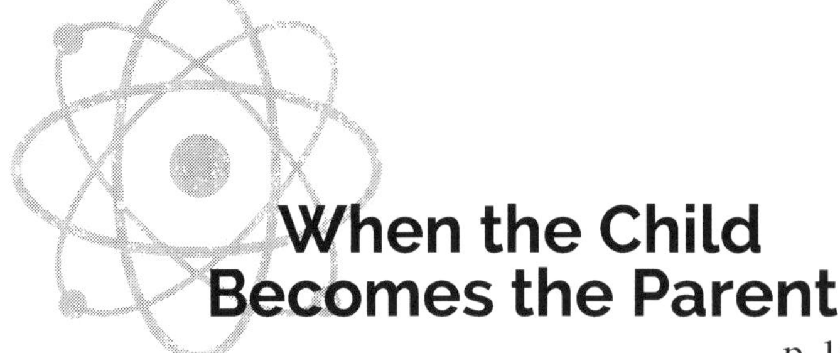

When the Child Becomes the Parent

p. 143-145

People are living longer, and the relationships we have with our parents will change over the years — and may even reverse.

If your and/or your partner's parents are still alive, what examples are you providing for your own children when they see you interact with them?

Have you and your parents had discussions about decisions that might need to be made in the future? Are you comfortable with arrangement? Why or why not? If not, what will you do to improve this?

Do you have all the information you would need in an emergency?

Are there family situations that might become difficult if your parents pass away or are incapacitated? How can they best be addressed?

Do you know where vital information, valuable items, wills, etc. are located? Do you know what to do for them in case you become responsible for your parent's care?

If your parents are no longer living, what are some of your favorite stories of them you'd like to share with your children?

Our Child's Journey

p. 146

The best legacy we can leave is by raising a productive, self-sufficient member of society who thrives and has the ability to support others in achieving their dreams.

Describe three specific investments you've made in your children.

1. ______________________________

____

2. ______________________________

____

3. ______________________________

____

Are you satisfied with this, or are there areas where you believe you should do more? If so, what are they and what will you do to correct this?

____

____

____

____

____

Minding Our Business and Our Finances

Financial knowledge, skills and focus are essential to building success and peace of mind.

Money, or the lack of it, can become a major source of stress in all parts of our lives. That's why it's crucial to focus on handling our finances and excelling at building our personal wealth.

Likewise, our careers also determine much of our happiness and fulfillment. Career and finance intertwine, and successful people pay close attention to both.

Skills and Vision

p. 148-149

While some might find their passion early on, few school-age children know what they want out of life. The adults around them are often little help because they also lack a clear vision of their own life's goals.

How has money influenced the decisions you've made in your life?

What mistakes did your parents make with money as you were growing up? Did you learn from their mistakes or do you find yourself repeating them?

What are your plans for retirement? Be specific.

Freedom and Independence: The "Why" of Business and Finance

p. 150-151

Is it easy to do the things that will build a successful career and lead to financial independence? Of course not. Is it worth it? Speaking for myself and my mentors, we couldn't dream of any other way to live.

In your life, what would freedom and independence look like? Dream, but be specific what your life could be for yourself and your family if you had financial independence.

Our Relationship with Money

p. 152

We all have a personal relationship with money, but we seldom examine how that relationship influences our decisions.

What are the primary emotions you connect with money?
Why are these the emotions that come to your mind?

____

____

____

____

____

____

Compare the financial and the psychic income you receive from your career.
Is the balance to your liking, or do you desire something to change? If so, what?

____

____

____

____

____

Money and Morality

p. 153

It can be hard to aspire to build a career and material wealth if a little voice is constantly telling you that amassing wealth is a bad thing.

What are some of the negative stereotypes you hold about rich/successful people? What was your parents' view of these people?

What deep-set attitudes about money might you need to change to achieve the success you want?

Find Someone Who's Done It

p. 154-157

...one of the best things we can do, both for ourselves and our families, is to connect with a business and finance mentor. We must find someone who can teach us, answer our questions and model the behaviors, actions and disciplines it takes to be happy and prosperous.

Describe your saving philosophy. Are you doing what you think you should to budget and save for the future? If not, why not?

____

____

____

What steps can you take to get to where you believe you should be financially?

____

____

____

Do you save 10 percent of your earnings each month, so you reinvest in your growth? If not, what is your plan to improve this?

____

____

____

In your workplace or other organizations you belong to, are there complacent people who dampen your drive or enthusiasm? Are there people who make it more difficult for you to give your all? Who are they? What impact do they have on you?

Describe the role of education in your life. Are you continuing to learn new things? Are you open to new approaches to challenges?

Think about your five closest friends — what impact have they had on your financial/business/motivational mindset?

1.

2.

3.

4.

5.

The Changing Role of Risk

p. 158-159

Many great leaders have ultimately prospered by taking calculated risks — and that means failing from time to time.

What is your personal definition of "risk" and "failure"?

How have these concepts changed for you over the years? How have they held you back? How can you use them to drive yourself forward?

Younger Generations and the Experienced Partner

p. 160

Once we've put together our circle of mentors and co-mentors, both older and younger, we can gather information and their advice. We can allow them to give us a broader view of the world.

Who are some younger mentors or potential mentors in your life who could teach you something or have taught you lessons or skills?

What are some topics that would you like to learn from a younger person to improve your career or your life?

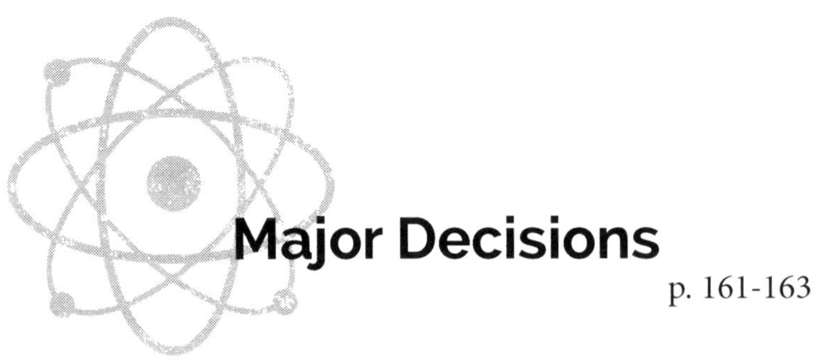

Major Decisions

p. 161-163

"You're older than you've ever been, and you're as young as you'll ever be."

Recall a life-altering decision you made. What factors did you take into account? What was your decision?

Looking back, do you believe your decision was the correct one? What did you learn? What would you do differently? Why?

The Struggles That Strengthen Us

p. 164

High achievers understand that it's important to use our struggles to build ourselves up instead of letting them drag us down to the point where we forget our dreams.

Recall a difficult time in your life. Setting aside the immediate struggles and difficulties, what positives were you able to pull from it as you look back?

The Clarity in Setting Goals

p. 165-171

We can't hit a target we haven't clearly defined. It's like taking a vacation with no destination in mind.

Describe a dream you want to achieve. Be specific. Visualize it as if you've already achieved it.

Now, break that dream down into big pieces (long-term thinking).

Break those long-term pieces into smaller, short-term pieces. Keep going until you have achievable goals and a clear timeline. (Keep S.M.A.R.T. — Specific, Measurable, Achievable, Relevant and Timely — in mind)

Specific: ______________________________

____

Measurable: ______________________________

____

Achievable: ______________________________

____

Relevant: ______________________________

____

Timely: ______________________________

____

What are some actions that might be uncomfortable for you? Why? What can you do to take these steps anyway?

____

____

____

How can you consistently remind yourself of your short- and long-term goals?

____

____

Checking Our Financial Attitudes

p. 172-175

By overcoming obstacles, we discover who we are and what we're made of. We must use our passion, enthusiasm, belief, focus, care and creativity to maintain the mental fortitude that will steer us through life's difficulties.

Does your circle of friends support your dreams/goals? If so, how?

____

____

Examine your goals — why do you *really* want to achieve these goals?

____

____

What do you need to work on to prepare yourself for achieving your goals?

____

____

____

Being truthful with yourself, are you *truly* hungry or are you comfortable?

____

____

How can you set the stage for your next short-term goal?
What can you do *today* to smooth the path forward?

___

___

___

What are some potential challenges or roadblocks between you and your goal, and how can you overcome them?

___

___

___

What kind of continuing education/training will you need? How can you best get it?

___

___

What are some of your self-imposed limits? How real are they?
How can they be set aside or overcome?

___

___

How have your plans changed over the years? Are your stated dreams still the best fit for you, or has your life evolved to the point where they should be re-imagined?

___

___

___

Our Calling

p. 176-177

> *...it's crucial to find the purpose — our "why" — that drives our lives, and make sure it provides us with happiness and fulfillment; if it doesn't, it's not our purpose. This is not a selfish question.* We can't love others if we don't love ourselves.

What are you core values and beliefs?

____

____

____

What do you truly want to show for your life's work and effort?

____

____

____

How might you change your life if money was no object?

____

____

____

____

We Are In Sales

p. 178-184

The toughest sale we will ever have is selling ourselves. If we don't believe in ourselves, our product and our idea, no one else will believe, either.

Name several moments in your everyday life when you have to "sell" (an idea, action, product, etc.).

____

____

____

Describe the last time you had exceptional sales experience (either as the seller or the buyer).

____

____

____

What is your sales style? What are you doing to continually improve it?

____

____

____

____

Think of the jargon associated with your career. Are there common words that could be substituted to explain things to an outsider more clearly? Come up with examples.

In a sales situation, do you sell yourself first? Notice the body language you use in your next conversation. Were there any surprises?

What are some ways you can boost the value of the product/service/idea that you're trying to sell, instead of dropping the price?

Think of a natural, non-pushy way to explain to people what you do. Is it simple?

____

____

____

____

Circles of Confidence

In what areas (either in your career or your life) are you an expert?

____

____

____

What are your natural strengths?

____

____

____

____

Have you ever "leaned away" from these strengths at work or other areas of your life? If so, why do you think you did this?

____

____

____

Training Ourselves to Lead Others

p. 185-192

The best leaders I've ever known have seen their role as an opportunity to serve others. Where average-to-poor managers seek to take advantage of the situation, great leaders have a code of ethics and the desire to watch and support their team members grow and prosper.

Do you consider yourself a "natural" leader? Why or why not?

Think back to the best and worst leaders you've had.
Why specifically do you consider them this way?

Think of the role that conflict plays in your workplace. Is it healthy or destructive? What steps can you take to make it productive?

Consider your workplace. Are any of the seven culture killers (big ego, micromanaging, gossip, office politics, dishonesty/lack of transparency, lack of recognition and unresolved issues) present? What will you do from where you are to confront them?

Steps to a Prosperous Life

p. 193-198

Billionaires think differently than millionaires and millionaires think differently than broke people. Healthy people have a different outlook than sick people, and happy people unquestionably view the world differently than miserable people.

How can you show your appreciation to the ones in your life who deserve it the most? Who are they and how do/will you show your appreciation?

Name a moment when conflict actually created chemistry.
What did you do to make that happen?

What one thing have you done (or are going to do) today to achieve a short- or long-term goal?

Do you have a regular budget? What are some of the everyday situations where money gets away from you? How will you fix that?

Are you financially situated for retirement? If you lived to 100, would you be able to survive financially? What would your 100-year-old self want to tell your present-day self?

Do you have a will? If so, is it up to date? Would your loved ones be prepared with all the information they need if you were to die today? Are all your documents in place? If not, what steps will you take everything is properly prepared?

Examine the debt in your life and the place it takes up in your finances.
Does it fall into the "good" debt or "bad" debt category?

Be Extraordinary

p. 199

No one sets out to have an average life or average career. The decisions we make every step of the way, however, dictate the course of our lives.

If you were to die tomorrow, what are three dreams/goals you would most regret not accomplishing?

1. ______________________________

____

2. ______________________________

____

3. ______________________________

____

Since you're LIVING now and reading *The Theory of 5*, what steps will you take to make these goals come true?

1. ______________________________

____

2. ______________________________

____

3. ______________________________

____

The Only Body We'll Ever Have

Good health is something that's easy to take for granted — until it's gone. It's actually the keystone to a great life. Without our health, every other aspect of The Theory of 5 becomes exponentially more difficult.

Our abilities, our energy, our very lives depend on good health habits. The longer we go without a plan to take care of our health, the harder it becomes to make changes to maintain our health as we get older.

Whether or not fitness and exercise come easy to us, it's important to not ignore or take our health for granted.
We must pay attention to our health.

It Can't Be Ignored

p. 202-203

For a while, youth can make up for poor exercise and eating habits. As we get older, however, time starts to take a toll on our bodies and we pay the price for our old, bad behaviors.

What is your health situation right now? Give yourself a letter grade (A, B, C, D or F). Explain your grade.

___

___

___

What would you like it to be? What do you aspire to when it comes to your health?

___

___

___

What steps will you take *today* to start the process?

___

___

___

Start Smart and Be Safe

p. 204

Don't be a "weekend warrior" who sits in a chair throughout the week and then launches into action on Saturday! That's a sure-fire way to injure yourself — or worse — and will put any plans you had for fitness on the back burner while you heal or recuperate.

When was your last comprehensive physical? What were the results?
Is it time for another?

____

____

____

What specific questions would you like to ask your doctor?
Write them down here so you don't forget to ask them while in the doctor's office.

____

____

____

____

____

____

Our One and Only

p. 205

Imagine if you were a 16-year-old and a wealthy person came to you and said, "Hey, listen. I'm going to buy you any new car you want. Price is not an issue. Say the word, and I'll have it in your driveway tomorrow." The catch? "That's the only vehicle you going to have for the rest of your life." *How would we take care of that vehicle?*

Where has the maintenance for your body been lacking?

___

___

___

___

How will you correct this? When?

___

___

___

___

___

___

Finding Those Who Will Challenge Us

p. 206-208

If we compare ourselves to average, we're only going to be slightly better than average. *If we compare ourselves to the elite, however, we start looking at things differently.*

Who would you like to emulate when it comes to physical fitness? How do you believe they got to be where they are? Could they be your accountability partner? If not, who could you be accountable to in this area?

____

____

____

____

____

What are some specific fitness goals you'd like to set for yourself?

____

____

____

____

____

Uncommon Common Sense

p. 209-210

We all know that we've got to treat our bodies well by exercising and getting proper nutrition. And yet, there are so many otherwise intelligent people in our society who just won't take these simple ideas to heart — until it might be too late.

Examine your daily habits. Are they conducive to a healthy lifestyle? Why or why not?

____

____

____

What are your sleeping habits? Do you believe you get enough sleep/restful sleep? If not, what will you do to correct this?

____

____

Do you have a plan when you go grocery shopping? If yes, what is it?
If not, what should it be?

____

____

____

____

Get Going Early

p. 211-212

Meetings run long, unexpected events pop up and our time can get pecked away until something has to give. If we've already put our body through its paces, our health won't be the thing that gets skipped.

Taking an objective look at your schedule, energy level, etc., when is the best time for you to exercise?

____

____

____

____

What are some ways you will avoid getting sidetracked by the day's activities to ensure you put your body through its paces?

____

____

____

____

____

Fitness and Our Children

p. 213

Children learn what they see their parents do. *If they see their parents sitting on the couch never doing any physical activity, that becomes their "normal." If they see their parents take an interest in their own health and make good choices, however, they're much more likely to model that behavior long after they've left home and have started making their own choices.*

What were your parents' example when it comes to physical fitness and exercise? Did this example help you or hurt you?

____

____

____

____

What is your example to your own children? Will it help or hurt them as they grow?

____

____

____

____

____

Finding What Works for Us

p. 214

Getting fit isn't a "one-time" thing we can achieve and then move on. It's a constant process and a lifestyle decision. If it doesn't come easily or naturally, we need to design a plan and process that speaks to us.

What is your "Why" when it comes to exercise?

____

____

What activities do you enjoy doing? What activities would you like to continue to do as you get older?

____

____

____

____

What upcoming event could serve as a Mental Event Challenge (MEC) for you?

____

____

____

____

Listening to Our Bodies

p. 215

Aging is part of life; it's going to happen. Deciding to put in the effort to becoming and staying fit and healthy, however, is a life enhancement, *and one we can attain.*

How has your body changed in the past 10 years? In the past 20?

How have/will you adjust to these changes to keep yourself at maximum health?

Investing in Ourselves

p. 216

We shouldn't be afraid to invest in our health and in ourselves. What better investment could we make?

What are you ignorant about when it comes to exercise and physical fitness?

What would be most valuable lesson for you to learn to keep yourself in shape?

What would you tell your 20-year-younger self to do so you would have enjoyed better health today?

What do you think your 20-year-older self would tell you today? Be specific.

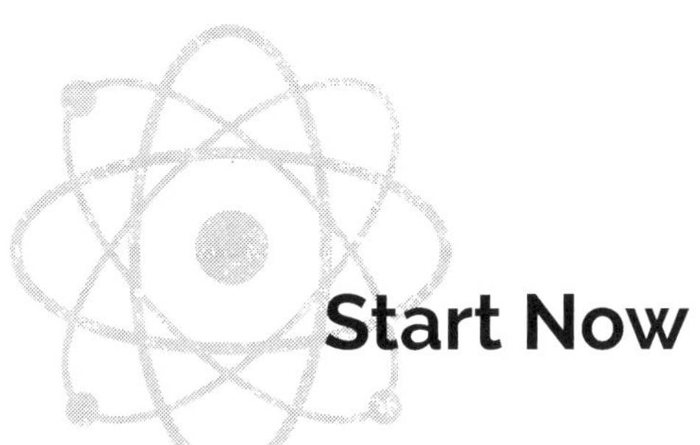

Start Now

p. 217

I've heard people say they want to get in a little better shape before they go to the gym. That's a plan for failure if there ever was one. Even if we start with a 50-yard walk, starting something now *is what's important.*

What are some of your "go to" excuses when it comes to exercise and fitness?

____

____

____

____

____

What will you do to work around these excuses to get in better shape?

____

____

____

____

____

Interviews

Learning from the experience and wisdom of others is the cornerstone of The Theory of 5.

The people interviewed for The Theory of 5 *are living proof of how to live an exceptional life. The questions here are generated from their experiences in different areas of their lives.*

Take this opportunity to examine the areas of your own life and apply their wisdom to your own situation.

Dave Anderson

p. 221-226

"I knew the first couple of years would be difficult, and they were, but getting started is the hardest part. That's what it took, and you do what it takes."

Think of a time when you started something — a business, a new position, a new relationship, etc. Describe the fears and the hopes you had. What worked well for you? Now, having read *The Theory of 5*, what would you change to improve the results?

Think of a person who has wronged you, either lightly or gravely. Is it possible for you to forgive them? What would that forgiveness mean for them? What would it mean for you?

Dale Pollak

p. 227-229

"I tell my people all the time that 'our best days are ahead.' That credo works in both good times and bad."

Name something about yourself that you believe is holding you back. How can this limitation, with The Theory of 5 mindset, instead be used to propel you forward?

____

____

____

____

____

What one lesson from The Theory of 5 do you want your children to take from you when they look back on their own lives?

____

____

____

____

____

Evelyn Longsworth

p. 230-235

"It's also important to know where your mate is emotionally. What is he really feeling? What's he experiencing? How is his career going? And all of that comes back to communicating, and I think you have to talk sooner than later."

What specific actions or behaviors do you use to show your child you believe in them?

Describe ways in which you and your partner are a team. What are some specific actions or behaviors you use to show that you support them?

Jerry H. Pyle

p. 236-241

"The biggest danger, though, is to overuse numbers and hide the most valuable information."

In a business setting, how do you separate the important information and activities from what can be delayed or ignored? How effective are you at this?

When is the last time you've handwritten a letter to someone — a family member, your partner or a friend? What effect do you believe this would have on them?

David Boice

p. 242-248

"We have a saying in my family: 'Change, whether good or bad, is resisted with equal intensity.'"

Describe your attitude toward change, either big or small. What steps can you take to develop a Theory of 5 mindset that more embraces adaptability and innovation?

____

____

____

____

____

What risks — physical, emotional or otherwise — are you prepared to let your child take? How does this attitude support or hinder their personal development?

____

____

____

____

____

Chip Perry

p. 249-252

"You can't skim across the top of an issue; you've got to dive down into the data and see what the underlying problems are — and what the underlying opportunities are."

Describe the role of curiosity as you've traveled your career path.
Are you more or less curious about personal and professional growth than those around you? How has this affected your life?

____

____

____

____

____

What is a physical activity you enjoy, and how can you tailor a health and fitness routine to make the most of this activity?

____

____

____

____

____

Susan Givens

p. 253-256

"Successful people don't give in to anger or frustration. They stay humble and think it out before moving forward."

How do you react in general to stressful situations in the workplace?
Is this reaction effective, or could it be improved upon?

____

____

____

____

____

Describe ways in which you are or have been your child's advocate in various situations.

____

____

____

____

____

____

Lee Kemp

p. 257-260

"My philosophy of fitness is to die healthy. If God blesses me with old age, I want to be healthy as long as I live."

As you've aged, how has your body changed? Have these changes kept you from doing things you used to enjoy? What will you do to compensate or change your fitness routine to take back these activities?

What are some habits you will change to increase your health and fitness level?

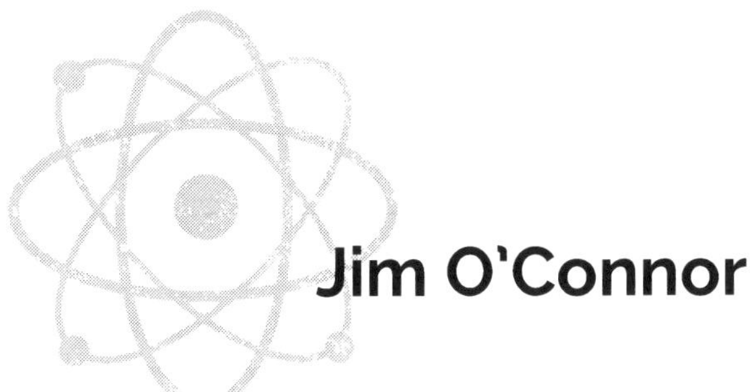

Jim O'Connor

p. 261-265

"You can't just put up a slide on January 1 and say, 'Okay, here's the strategy' and hope the organization understands it. You've got to constantly reinforce your strategy through good communication.*"*

Either as a leader or a team member, how clear are you on both your vision and the company's vision? What questions will you ask yourself or others to increase this clarity?

____

____

____

____

____

Describe the different roles you and your partner take on when it comes to raising your children. Are you both comfortable in these roles? What areas could or should be reassigned?

____

____

____

____

____

Grant Cardone

p. 266-273

"We don't talk to our kids about success. They see success happening in our family."

Taking an objective look at your career, do you believe you are on the right path to achieve your goals and vision? Why or why not? What adjustments or changes would get you closer to your objectives?

Your children are always watching you. Name five specific examples you are setting for them that you are proud of when they witness your interactions with the world.

1.

2.

3.

4.

5.

Sean Wolfington

p. 274-282

"For me, spirituality is the trunk of the tree, and everything else is the branches growing from that center. My faith is almost like oxygen — what oxygen is to my body is what faith is to my soul."

As a leader or team member, what are some ways you make a difference in the lives of your co-workers, team members and customers?

What are some specific ways your faith or spirituality play out in your day-to-day life?

Afterword

Life as It Should Be

p. 284-286

Imagine a world where we are clearly aware of our PURPOSE — and we have the passion and determination to live it. Envision what will happen when we live a Theory of 5 life.

Taking a look at your weekly schedule:

Are you in a satisfying line of work? If not, what is your plan to improve this?

____

____

Are you seeing enough of your loved ones? If not, what is your plan to change this?

____

____

Are you able to pursue your passions?
If yes, give a specific example. If not, what is your plan?

____

____

Are you living up to your potential? Why or why not?

____

____

What five steps can you take *today* to start living a Theory of 5 life?

1.

2.

3.

4.

5.

What mentors do you need to seek out to befriend and ask them to guide you on your Theory of 5 journey?

Name: ______________________________ To5 Area: __________

Reason: ____

____

Name: ______________________________ To5 Area: __________

Reason: ____

____

Name: ______________________________ To5 Area: __________

Reason: ____

____

Name: ______________________________ To5 Area: __________

Reason: ____

____

Name: ______________________________ To5 Area: __________

Reason: ____

____

About the Authors

Chris Saraceno is a business executive, real estate investor, speaker and leader who has, over the past 36 years, *discovered what surrounding yourself with the happy and prosperous people, coupled with hard work, can bring over a lifetime.*

A vice president and partner in the Kelly Automotive Group and founder of the online community DealerElite.com, Chris has built the skills necessary during his career to motivate individuals and teams to achieve goals they wouldn't have otherwise thought possible. By having mentors — and being a mentor to others — Chris has learned a secret of most successful individuals: You don't have to do it alone.

Chris has been a featured speaker at numerous conventions and has published hundreds of articles both online and in business magazines. While he speaks on a wide range of topics, the goal of all this activity is the same: to assist people in achieving their potential and live their best life.

Chris lives in Merritt Island, Florida with his wife, Lisa, and boxer dog, Apollo. He has four children and six grandchildren. He is committed to giving all of them his best energy and guidance, and to providing an example of what will be accomplished when you have support and an exceptional attitude.

For more information, visit www.TheoryOf5.com or www.ChrisSaraceno.com.

David Falkirk Davis is a writer, editor and former journalist. He lives in Indiana with his wife, Kristen. David is also a fiction writer and is the author of the *The Joined World* trilogy, The *Death Effect* and the *Fast 40* series of flash fiction. For more information, visit www.DavidFalkirk.com.

Made in the USA
Middletown, DE
03 August 2022